discover more
World Religions
What Is Hinduism?

Ernest Brazzos

IN ASSOCIATION WITH

Published in 2026 by Britannica Educational Publishing (a trademark of Encyclopædia Britannica, Inc.) in association with The Rosen Publishing Group, Inc.
2544 Clinton Street, Buffalo, NY 14224

Copyright © 2026 by Encyclopædia Britannica, Inc. Britannica, Encyclopædia Britannica, and the Thistle logo are registered trademarks Encyclopædia Britannica, Inc. All rights reserved.

Rosen Publishing materials copyright © 2026 The Rosen Publishing Group, Inc. All rights reserved.

Distributed exclusively by Rosen Publishing.
To see additional Britannica Educational Publishing titles, go to rosenpublishing.com.

All rights reserved. No part of this book may be reproduced in any form without permission in writing from the publisher, except by a reviewer.

Editor: Greg Roza
Book Design: Michael Flynn

Photo Credits: Cover The Captured Creations/Shutterstock.com; (series background) Dai Yim/Shutterstock.com; p. 4 tscreationz/Shutterstock.com; p. 5 Roman Babakin/Shutterstock.com; p. 6 Nila Newsom/Shutterstock.com; p. 7 szefei/Shutterstock.com; p. 9 Dutt Swapnil/Shutterstock.com; p. 10 Ritu Manoj Jethani/Shutterstock.com; p. 11 StockImageFactory.com/Shutterstock.com; p. 12 Sallehudin Ahmad/Shutterstock.com; p. 13 meunierd/Shutterstock.com; p. 15 (top) reddees/Shutterstock.com; p. 15 (bottom) Nature Clickz/Shutterstock.com; p. 17 (top) Nature people game etc/Shutterstock.com; p. 17 (bottom) rasika108/Shutterstock.com; p. 18 Priti sinha 12345/Shutterstock.com; p. 19 backpacker79/Shutterstock.com; p. 21 (top) phive/Shutterstock.com; p. 21 (bottom) Parikh Mahendra N/Shutterstock.com; p. 23 mdsharma/Shutterstock.com; p. 24 https://commons.wikimedia.org/wiki/File:Portrait_of_Raja_Ram_Mohun_Roy,_1833.jpg; p. 25 https://commons.wikimedia.org/wiki/File:Mahatma-Gandhi,_studio,_1931.jpg; p. 27 (top) Cavan-Images/Shutterstock.com; p. 27 (bottom) Jaclyne Ortiz/Shutterstock.com; p. 28 RuslanKphoto/Shutterstock.com; p. 29 Ground Picture/Shutterstock.com.

Cataloging-in-Publication Data

Names: Brazzos, Ernest.
Title: What is Hinduism? / Ernest Brazzos.
Description: New York : Britannica Educational Publishing, in association with Rosen Educational Services, 2026. | Series: Discover more: world religions | Includes glossary and index.
Identifiers: ISBN 9781641904612 (library bound) | ISBN 9781641904605 (pbk) | ISBN 9781641904629 (ebook)
Subjects: LCSH: Hinduism--Juvenile literature.
Classification: LCC BL1203.B74 2026 | DDC 294.5--dc23

Manufactured in the United States of America

Some of the images in this book illustrate individuals who are models. The depictions do not imply actual situations or events.

CPSIA Compliance Information: Batch #CSBRIT26. For further information contact Rosen Publishing at 1-800-237-9932.

Contents

An Ancient Religion 4
Hindu Beliefs 6
Hindu Practices 10
Major Hindu Gods 14
Lesser Gods 18
How Hindus Celebrate 20
Hindu History 22
Hinduism Today 26
Glossary 30
For More Information 31
Index 32

An Ancient Religion

Hinduism was founded more than 4,000 years ago, making it one of the world's oldest religions. Over the centuries, however, its followers—called Hindus—have accepted many new ideas and combined them with the old ones. More than nine hundred million people practice Hinduism worldwide. Most of them live in India, where Hinduism began.

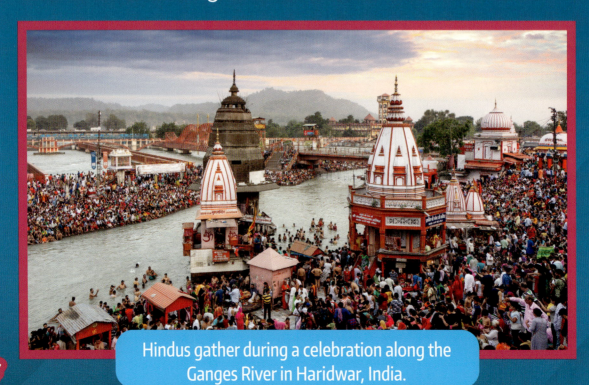

Hindus gather during a celebration along the Ganges River in Haridwar, India.

This ancient Hindu temple is in Vietnam. It was built in the fourth century.

Hinduism is different from other major religions because it has no founder. Its origins are lost in the distant past. It has several religious texts rather than one major text. No one has set down a list of beliefs for all Hindus to follow. Hinduism is diverse in belief and practice. Many sects and schools of philosophy coexist within Hinduism.

Consider This

Hinduism has no single founder. Other major religions, including Judaism, Christianity, and Islam, are well known for their founders. Do you think having a founder makes religious worship different?

Hindu Beliefs

The Veda is an ancient body of sacred Hindu writings. The word Veda means "knowledge." Hindus composed these texts in what is now India over hundreds of years, beginning in about 1500 BCE. For a long time, people passed down the texts of the Veda by **reciting** them. Eventually they wrote the texts down. Hindus today still study the Veda.

The religious student is reading an older form of the Veda recorded on thin pieces of wood. The Veda can also be read in a modern book format.

An Indian woman in traditional clothes prays during the Hindu celebration of Diwali, the Festival of Lights.

Hindus believe in a spiritual power called Brahman. Brahman is the source of all life and is present in everything and every place. The human soul, called atman, is part of the universal Brahman. Hindus generally believe that when someone dies, the atman is reborn in another body.

WORD WISE

RECITING MEANS TO REPEAT SOMETHING, SUCH AS A POEM OR FABLE, FROM MEMORY. MANY ANCIENT STORIES, HISTORIES, AND RELIGIOUS PASSAGES WERE ORIGINALLY PASSED DOWN TO NEW GENERATIONS THROUGH SPOKEN WORDS.

A soul may return many times in human, animal, or even plant form. This idea is known as reincarnation. The idea of karma says that what a person does in the present life will affect the next life. The cycle of rebirth continues until one accepts that the atman (the individual soul) and Brahman (the universal soul) are one. Most Hindus consider breaking free from this cycle of rebirth to be a person's highest purpose.

Hindus are expected to follow the rule of ahimsa, which means "nonviolence" in Sanskrit, an ancient language of India. This means that one must never wish to harm anyone or anything. Hindus consider many animals to be sacred. Devout Hindus do not eat meat.

A guru is a spiritual teacher or guide in Hinduism. Some gurus have founded their own sects, or schools, of Hinduism. Some sects consider the guru as a personification of a god living among Hindus. The word guru means "venerable," or "honorable," in Sanskrit.

According to Hindu texts, Nandi is the bull god who serves as a mount to the god Shiva. In many Hindu communities, cows and bulls are considered sacred and allowed to roam freely.

Consider This
Why do you think Hindus do not eat cows or other animals?

Hindu Practices

Puja, the act of worshipping, can take different forms, from short daily rites in the home to long rituals in temples. In general, Hindus pray for a god to enter their home or a temple, and then treat the god as an honored guest. Temples vary from small village shrines to huge complexes—almost small cities—with walled courtyards, pools for ceremonial bathing, schools, hospitals, and **monasteries**. Religious services are not held at particular times, as they are in many other religions.

Hindus perform rituals and hold festivals in temples. This temple in Robbinsville, New Jersey, is one of the largest Hindu temples in the world!

This family is celebrating the Hindu holiday Diwali in their home.

The first act of temple worship is opening the temple door. Temple visitors may meditate or chant. Images or icons of the gods, called murti or pratima, are honored with gifts of flowers, fruit, or perfumes. Visiting worshippers are given small portions of holy food. Many Hindus also worship at home.

WORD WISE
MONASTERIES ARE PLACES WHERE RELIGIOUS PEOPLE CALLED MONKS LIVE, WORK, STUDY, AND PRAY.

The Hindu search for spiritual knowledge and for release from the cycle of rebirth is known as Tantrism. It involves chanting sacred sounds and words called mantras and drawing symbols called mandalas.

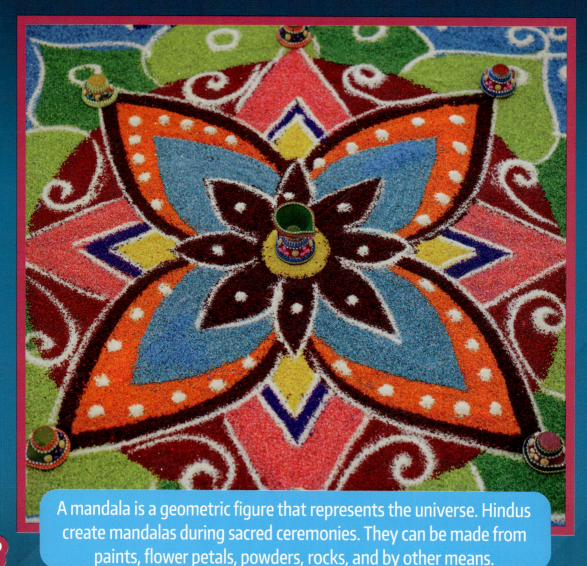

A mandala is a geometric figure that represents the universe. Hindus create mandalas during sacred ceremonies. They can be made from paints, flower petals, powders, rocks, and by other means.

Hindus scatter the ashes from a cremation on the river, believing that the dead will avoid the cycle of rebirth and go straight to heaven.

Pilgrimages, or journeys to holy places, have been important in Hinduism since ancient times. Many pilgrimage sites lie in northern India along the Ganges River, which Hindus consider the holiest of rivers. They call it Mother Ganges. Hindus believe that the Ganges River is holy. They bathe in its water to purify themselves. People have built many temples along the Ganges for cremating, or burning, the dead.

Consider This

Why do religious followers make pilgrimages to holy places? Can you think of any holy places in other religions, like Islam or Christianity?

Major Hindu Gods

The worship of the gods Vishnu, Shiva, and Shakti make up the three major branches of modern Hinduism. Followers of Hinduism believe that the gods sometimes take on human or animal form. These forms of the gods are called avatars.

The god Vishnu is considered the protector and preserver of life. In Sanskrit his name means "The Pervader." The worship of Vishnu and his avatars is called Vaishnavism. The most popular avatars of Vishnu are Krishna and Rama. Images of Vishnu often show him with his wife, Lakshmi.

The branch of Hinduism that is devoted to Shiva is called Shaivism. The god Shiva represents the forces that create life as well as those that destroy it. The name Shiva is Sanskrit for "Auspicious One." Shiva takes different forms—such as a wandering beggar, a person who is half man and half female, or a dancer.

Vishnu is usually depicted with blue skin and four arms and holding symbolic items in each hand.

compare and contrast

Unlike Hindus, followers of Christianity and Judaism worship only one god. Can you think of some similarities between Hinduism and Judaism or Christianity?

The tallest statue of Shiva, shown here, is in Suryabinayak, Nepal. It is 143 feet (43.6 m) tall.

Shakti is the supreme goddess of Hinduism. Like the god Shiva, Shakti can be either kind or fierce, depending on her form. As Parvati, she is a kind and beautiful woman. As Kali, she is a fierce giantess with black skin, a bloodred tongue, and large tusks. Kali carries an assortment of weapons and wears a necklace of human skulls. As mother goddess, Shakti stands for all aspects of nature, from birth to death. The worship of Shakti is called Shaktism.

Brahma (not to be confused with Brahman) is considered the creator of the universe. In ancient times, he was widely worshipped, but his following is now small. Brahma is usually shown with four arms and four heads.

This statue shows Shakti as Kali taunting those who view her.

compareandcontrast

How are Vishnu, Shiva, and Shakti similar? How are they different?

Brahma is the creator god of Hinduism.

17

Lesser Gods

Many Hindu sources say that there are 33 Hindu gods, but other sources differ. Ganesa (or Ganesha) is the elephant headed son of Shiva and Shakti. He is prayed to before beginning a task or project. Lakshmi, the wife of Vishnu, is the goddess of wealth. Sarasvati is the goddess of learning and the arts. Hanuman is the monkey god associated with the adventures of Rama. In some areas of India, people worship Manasa, the goddess of snakes.

Hindu gods often have features of both humans and animals. Ganesa is part human and part elephant in most depictions.

Monkeys are considered holy in Hinduism. Hanuman, shown here, is a monkey god.

Many animals and plants are also regarded as sacred in Hinduism. Hindus believe the cow is especially sacred. All cattle are protected, and even Hindus who are not vegetarian do not eat beef. Monkeys and some snakes are also holy.

Consider This

Many Hindus are vegetarians who are restricted from eating meat. Do other religions put restrictions on what can be eaten? Can you think of an example?

How Hindus Celebrate

Hindu celebrations include religious ceremonies, music, and dances. Festivals take place throughout the year and often last many days. Diwali is probably the most popular Hindu holiday. It is a New Year celebration that lasts for five days in late October or early November. Diwali is celebrated by exchanging presents, eating festive meals, visiting friends, and lighting lamps and fireworks.

Another important festival is Holi. It is a spring festival. People throw colored water and powder on one another, and traditional roles are reversed. Sharad Navratri is a Hindu festival that takes place in early autumn, usually over nine days. The festival celebrates the goddesses Durga, Lakshmi, and Sarasvati. It often ends with the Dussehra celebration on the 10th day. Dussehra marks the victory of Rama over the ten-headed demon king Ravana. People in southern India celebrate the harvest festival of Pongal in January.

Diwali is the Hindu festival of lights. Hindus light clay oil lamps called diyas. The light represents the triumph of good over evil.

compare and contrast

Most cultures and religions celebrate the New Year with special customs and festivals. How is Diwali similar to or different from other New Year celebrations?

Holi is the Hindu festival of color. Hindus gather around bonfires to sing and dance.

Hindu History

Around 1500 BCE, a group of people from what is now Iran invaded India. They had a religion, called Vedism, that involved making animal **sacrifices** to the gods. They wrote the oldest parts of the Veda. Vedism was the starting point of Hinduism.

Over the years, the influence of other peoples and ideas made Hinduism a very different religion from Vedism. People began to disapprove of the killing of animals as sacrifices. The older gods of Vedism were slowly replaced by newer ones. But some rites of Vedism have survived in modern Hinduism.

In the 1000s, Muslims invaded northern India. Islam, the religion of the Muslims, influenced some new schools of Hinduism. In the late 1400s, a new religion called Sikhism combined parts of Hinduism and Islam.

Great Britian claimed India as a colony in the early 1800s. Hinduism helped unify, or bring together, the people of India against the British.

Dashavatara Temple in Deogarh, India, is one of the oldest Hindu temples that is still standing. It was likely built between 600 and 700 CE.

WORD WISE
A SACRIFICE IS AN OFFERING TO A GOD. OFTEN, THIS MEANS THE KILLING OF AN ANIMAL.

During the period of British colonialism in India, however, some Hindu leaders began speaking out against parts of traditional Hinduism. The reformer Ram Mohun Roy, for example, spoke out against the ancient form of social organization called the caste system. Under this system, people were treated differently depending on which social class they were born into. The reformers used some Western ideas to modernize Hinduism.

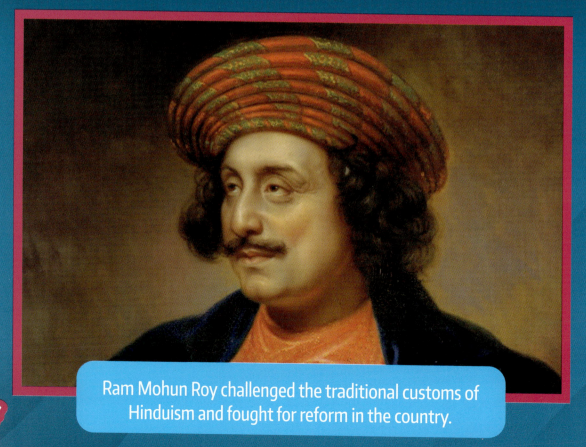

Ram Mohun Roy challenged the traditional customs of Hinduism and fought for reform in the country.

Gandhi's nonviolent methods included boycotting, not buying, British goods, and staging peaceful protests and marches.

The most famous Hindu leader of the 1900s was Mohandas Gandhi. He brought the idea of ahimsa into politics. He helped win India's independence from Britian using nonviolent methods.

Consider This
India has religions other than Hinduism. They include Buddhism, Sikhism, and Islam, among others. Do you think having multiple religions is good for the population and culture of a country?

Hinduism Today

A majority of the world's Hindus live in India. Today, India has a population of more than one billion people. More than three-fourths of the people living in India are Hindu. As the population of India continues to grow, so too will the influence of Hinduism.

The migration of Hindus has spread the beliefs and practices of Hinduism around the world. Since the 19th century, large Hindu communities have formed in Africa, Malaysia, the islands of the Pacific Ocean and the Indian Ocean, and some islands of the West Indies. Since World War II, many Hindus have settled in the United Kingdom and in the United States.

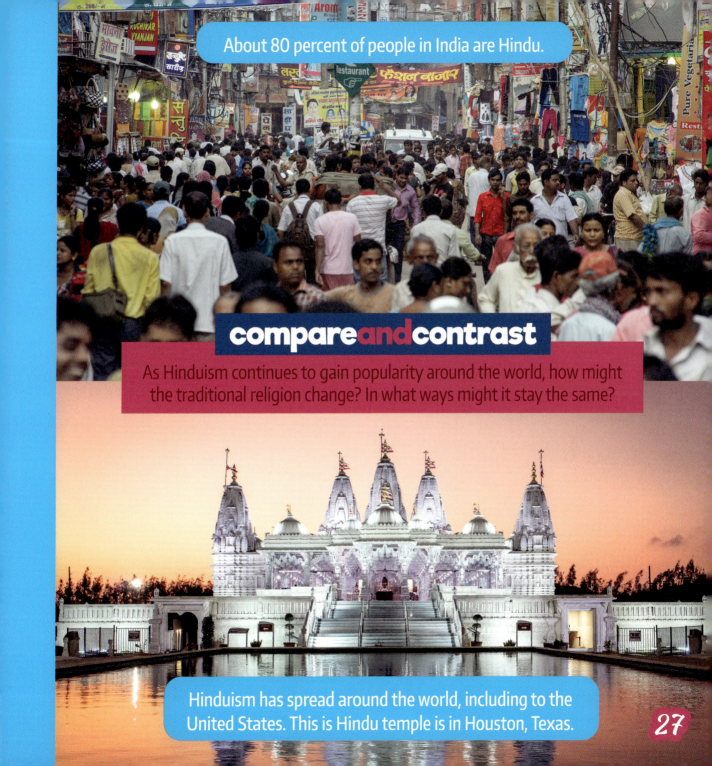

About 80 percent of people in India are Hindu.

compare and contrast

As Hinduism continues to gain popularity around the world, how might the traditional religion change? In what ways might it stay the same?

Hinduism has spread around the world, including to the United States. This is Hindu temple is in Houston, Texas.

Many of Hinduism's customs and traditions are appealing to many people and has influenced many cultures around the world. Yoga and **meditation** are popular in the United States and in many other countries. Yoga is a system of training for the body and the mind. The word yoga means "union" in Sanskrit.

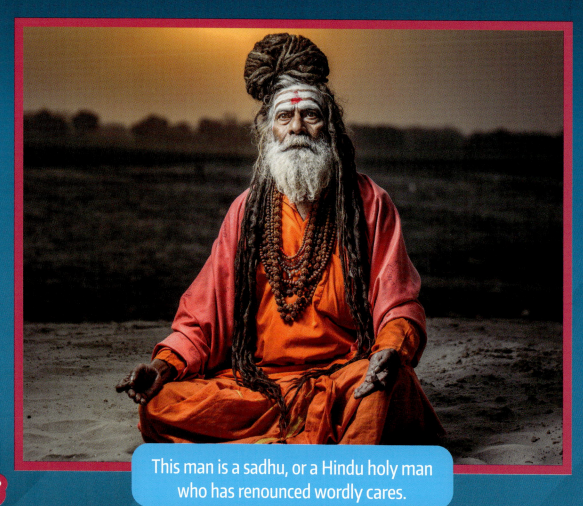

This man is a sadhu, or a Hindu holy man who has renounced wordly cares.

Yoga has become very popular in Western cultures. It promotes both physical and mental health.

Hindus practice yoga to feel united with a higher power. They seek this union through posture (the position of the body), breathing, diet, and meditation. Today, many people who do not follow Hinduism practice yoga for exercise and relaxation.

WORD WISE
MEDITATION IS A MENTAL EXERCISE WHERE A PERSON SITS QUIETLY AND FOCUSES ON THEIR BREATH. PEOPLE DO THIS TO RELAX, TO CLEAR THE MIND, AND TO REACH A HIGHER LEVEL OF AWARENESS.

Glossary

auspicious Showing or suggesting that future success is likely.
ceremonial Involved in a ceremony or religious event.
chant To speak with little or no change in tone.
coexist To live in peace with each other.
colony A territory under the control of a nation.
complex A collection of buildings.
devout Having a strong belief in a religion.
diverse Made up of many different parts.
mantra A sound, word, or phrase that is repeated by someone who is praying or meditating.
personification The representation of a thing or idea as a person.
pervade To be present throughout.
philosophy Basic beliefs about the way people should live.
reformers People who work to make something better.
revere To show devotion and honor to.
rites Important religious events or practices.
rituals Religious ceremonies.
sacred Holy; something important to a particular religion.
shrine A place of worship.
tusks Very long, large teeth that stick out when the mouth is closed.
universal Including everyone and everything.
vegetarian A person who refrains from eating meat and lives on a diet made up mostly of vegetables, fruits, grains, and nuts.

For More Information

Books

Ganeri, Anita. *Hindu Festivals and Traditions.* Mankato, MN: Pebble Books, 2025.

Buckley, James, Jr. *Gandhi: The Peaceful Protestor!* Ashland, OR: Portable Press, 2021.

Websites

Mohandas Gandhi
www.ducksters.com/biography/mohandas_gandhi.php
Read the biography of Mohandas Gandhi at the Ducksters website.

What Is Hinduism?
www.bbc.co.uk/bitesize/articles/zmpp92p
Learn more about Hinduism and view a short video about the religion.

Publisher's note to educators and parents: Our editors have carefully reviewed these websites to ensure that they are suitable for students. Many websites change frequently, however, and we cannot guarantee that a site's future contents will continue to meet our high standards of quality and educational value. Be advised that students should be closely supervised whenever they access the internet.

Index

A
ahimsa, 8, 25

B
Brahma, 16, 17
Brahman, 7, 8

D
Diwali, 7, 11, 20, 21

G
Gandhi, Mohandas, 25
Ganges River, 4, 13
guru, 8

H
Holi, 20, 21

I
India, 4, 6, 7, 8, 13, 18, 20, 22, 23, 24, 25, 26, 27

L
lesser gods, 18, 19

N
Nepal, 4, 15

R
reincarnation (cycle of rebirth), 8, 13
religious texts, 5, 6, 9
Roy, Ram Mohun, 24

S
sects (branches of Hinduism), 5, 8, 14
Shakti, 14, 16, 18
Shiva, 9, 14, 15, 16, 17, 18
Sikhism, 22, 25

T
temple, 5, 10, 11, 13, 23, 27

V
Veda, 6, 22
Vedism, 22
Vishnu, 14, 15, 17, 18

Y
yoga, 28, 29